IT WAS A
NIGHTMARE!

Compiled by Wendy Body and Pat Edwards

Acknowledgements

We are grateful to the following for permission to reproduce copyright material: Victor Gollancz Ltd for the story 'Fox Buster' from *Fox Busters* by Dick King-Smith; the author's agents for the story 'Dogs and Wolves and Hares and Foxes' from *Stories of Ancient Britain* by Margery Morris © Margery Morris 1977; the author, Brian Patten for his poem 'I Don't Believe in Human-Tales' from *Gargling with Jelly* (Viking Kestrel 1985); Viking Penguin Inc. for the story 'Victory?' from *The Eighteenth Emergency* by Betsy Byars Copyright © 1973 by Betsy Byars. Pages 14–19 were written by John Robottom and pages 50–1 were written by Bill Boyle.

We are grateful to the following for permission to reproduce photographs: British Museum, page 17 left; J. Allen Cash Ltd, 14, 15; Colchester & Essex Museums pages 19, 17 right (photo: Woodmansterne Picture Library); Thames Television, page 50, Puffin Books, page 51.

Illustrators, other than those acknowledged with story include: Gordon Fitchett pp. 4–5, 62–4; Frances Cony 6–13; Clyde Pearson pp. 14–35; Chris Price pp. 36–49, 51; Jones Sewell & Associates pp. 50–1; Peter Foster 52–61.

Contents

What's a Nightmare?

The monster is gaining on you . . . it's about to pounce . . .
you try to run but your legs won't work properly . . . in
desperation you start climbing a tree . . . the monster is
closer now . . . your heart is pounding . . . higher,
higher . . . it reaches out its ghastly hand,
grasping for your foot . . . panic-
stricken you back out along the
tree branch . . . CRACK!
It breaks — down you
fall . . . down . . .
down . . .

4

And you wake up in bed. Heart thumping? Mouth all dry?
Not quite sure where you are?

It's all right. You've just had a nightmare.

Why do we have nightmares? No one's quite sure, just as
scientists and medical people have been unable to agree on
why we dream. The usual explanation is that while we're
asleep our mind sorts out all the things we've seen, read
about, talked about or thought. Then it weaves a kind of
video tape in which these are all jumbled up. Usually if we
think hard about it, we'll find a clue somewhere in the
dream. Suppose you really did dream about a monster.
Well, you might have seen a movie about a monster a few
days earlier, you might have seen a shadow that looked like
a monster on the wall of the bathroom, or a school friend
might have told a joke about monsters . . .

Why some dreams are pleasant and others horrible and
scary — nightmares, in fact — no one knows. It could be
that something is worrying you, that you really are afraid.
Your mind could be turning your scared feeling about
tomorrow's maths test into a monster!

What about the name "nightmare"? Where did it come
from? Once, people believed that nightmares were actually
caused by a female monster that came and sat on your chest
while you were asleep. The word mare comes from an old
English word meaning "fiend", the kind that travelled at
night with witches.

And here's an interesting note. Mary Shelley saw her
Frankenstein monster in a nightmare she had one night. She
decided that what terrified her would terrify other people, so
the very next day she began to write what has become the
world's most famous horror story.

FOX BUSTER

Ransome, Sims and Jefferies were the three astonishing chickens who were to become a legend to future generations at Foxearth Farm. Not only could they fly out of the reach of foxes, but they found a way of defeating even the most crafty of attacks. Their deeds would be told in years to come by every hen to every brood of chicks, and by every vixen to every litter of foxcubs. For these three sisters were the Fox Busters.

Ransome, even more than her sisters, combined the finest qualities of her parents. Moreover she had inherited Spillers' shrewdness without that overlay of excessive caution with which her mother addressed every problem, and Massey-Harris's courage without the hot-headedness which was his trademark. More importantly, she was not simply better equipped than Sims and Jefferies. She knew she was. And most importantly, she was not conceited about this knowledge.

Increasingly, as the family and the rest of the flock waited for what all felt would be a fight to a finish, Ransome thought hard about the part she had to play, a part which she felt strongly would be vital. She could not of course know exactly what was in store for her but she knew, somehow, that she was destined for some final all-important struggle with the enemy.

So at roost-time, when all the head-scratching and preening and feather-settling was done, she perched and thought, long after the rest were sound asleep. Despite her proven skills, something had been worrying her for a long time now. Of her physical abilities she was not in any doubt. Just as the Foxearthers were vastly more skilled than ordinary fowls, and she and her sisters far superior to the rest of the flock, so she knew that in strength, speed, manoeuvrability, and accuracy she was the best. What worried her was the realisation that, despite all her great gifts she, like chickens everywhere, could not overcome the one great built-in fear; she was still, at heart, very frightened of foxes. And gradually, unavoidably, because she could not only out-act but also out-think the rest, she came to a conclusion. Like all truly brave individuals, she realised that the only way to fight fear is to look it in the face. She must go to the woods, find the foxes, confront them on their own ground. Only thus, she felt sure, could she build in herself that supreme confidence for the final act.

7

One morning then, her mind made up, she set off. She had done her greenhouse spell, eaten her extra grit and, particularly, laid that day's egg in flight on the rick-sheet range so as to go unarmed, trusting only in her powers of flight and her wits. She had said nothing of her plan to the rest, and made sure her departure was not noted. For lack of any better direction, she flew along the line of retreat which the four foxes had taken on that strange day when they had run about the farmyard in so odd a fashion. After flying for two or three miles, she suddenly saw below her exactly the kind of place for which she had been looking. It was a grassy clearing, as big as a football pitch, in the middle of the woods; and in the centre of the clearing stood a solitary beech tree; she glided towards it and pitched in the upper branches. Looking down, she saw that one great branch stuck out, parallel with the ground and about eight feet above it, just above fox-jump in fact; she dropped on to it, settled her feathers, and waited.

For a long time, nothing happened. Constantly swivelling her head, Ransome watched the circle of trees surrounding the clearing. Because, like all birds, she had no sense of smell, she had to rely on her eyes, and could not tell from the sharp stink, as a squirrel could have done, that there was already a fox hiding behind the beech's great trunk. He had run in a straight line from the wood, keeping the trunk between himself and the pullet. But before he could decide what next to do, the fringe of the clearing on the downwind side was suddenly alive with four, five, six pointed faces of long-noses drawn irresistibly by the breeze's message. And before long a dozen or more adult foxes and some part-grown cubs sat in a rough circle below Ransome's branch, and stared, and passed their tongues ceaselessly over their long white fangs.

This was the moment when any ordinary fowl would have panicked into a fluttering attempt at escape, or simply toppled, mesmerised, down into the jaws below. This was the moment, also, that Ransome was waiting for, had planned for, had thought about endlessly. Now she must look them in the eyes, each and every one of them, squarely and unflinchingly. And she did, sitting quite motionless except for the regular movement of her downbent head as one after another the foxes met her hard, cold, unblinking gaze, and one after another they dropped their eyes before the stare, some growling, some snarling a little, some whining in a kind of embarrassment.

9

Suddenly a big dog-fox, he who had hid behind the tree, ran and launched himself in a great leap at the pullet; but his teeth clacked together a yard below her claws, and all he got for his pains was a particularly icy and penetrating look followed by a huge yawn as Ransome opened her gape to its widest in a gesture of utter contempt.

At this the foxes' control broke, and one after another they ran and leapt and missed and leapt again, snarling and barking and even snapping at one another. One or two tried to climb the trunk of the tree, but the beech's smooth silvery skin did not give them enough hold to reach the crotch of the branch on which the maddening bird sat.

Newcomers came out of the woods, attracted by the rumpus, and eventually there were a couple of dozen long-nosed chicken lovers sitting, lying, or pacing restlessly beneath the branch. They began to talk among themselves, and though Ransome could not understand a word, Vulpine being a totally different language from Hennish, she listened to the horrid yowly voices and while she listened, planned her final move.

"Mum," said the biggest of the cubs to its mother, "it'll have to come down sooner or later, won't it? When it gets hungry or thirsty enough, I mean?"

"Silly child," was the reply. "That's a Foxearth fowl. They can fly. When it's ready, it'll just fly away."

"It doesn't make any noise, does it?" said another cub.

"Oh, they can't talk, like us. All the foolish things can do is squawk."

"Funny, though," said one of the other adult foxes, "this one somehow doesn't seem to be frightened of us. That's what annoys me about the stupid thing. Still I suppose it's worth waiting. There may be something wrong with it. I mean, what on my earth is it doing right out here, miles from the farm?"

Among the waiting pack were the four young raiders. Of all the foxes there, they, with the memory of their feast still fresh in their minds, were perhaps the most coldly furious at the sheer impudence of this solitary intruder into their country. One of them — one of the two vixens — walked forward until she stood directly beneath Ransome. Then she reared up on her hind legs, and in a thin jarring voice shaking with anger, she said, "I have a strange feeling that we shall meet again one day, you and I."

Ransome blinked owlishly, and the vixen dropped back on all fours with a low growl.

Ransome had now been sitting on the branch of the beech tree for nearly an hour, and thought it time to make for home. On the one hand she had proved to her own satisfaction that she was battleready, that she could stand the fire of those terrible green eyes without flinching. On the other hand she saw no point in prolonging the confrontation, for by now her absence from home would have been noticed and she did not want to worry the family: it was easy to imagine her father in his anxiety sending search-patrols all over the place and thus weakening the defences. However she did not wish to end the affair by simply taking the easy way out and flying effortlessly away from her enemies. While they had been talking, she had been thinking, and now at last the kind of opportunity for which she had been hoping presented itself.

The adult foxes had all stayed close by the tree, waiting, watchful for any possible chance which might reward their patience; but the cubs, like youngsters everywhere, became bored by inactivity and began a series of rough-and-tumble games out in the grass of the clearing. The biggest of the cubs however was all by itself, for it had discovered an interesting hole among the grass-roots and its nostrils were full of the smell of fieldmouse. With its back to the beech tree twenty yards away, and its long nose stuck down the mousehole, it

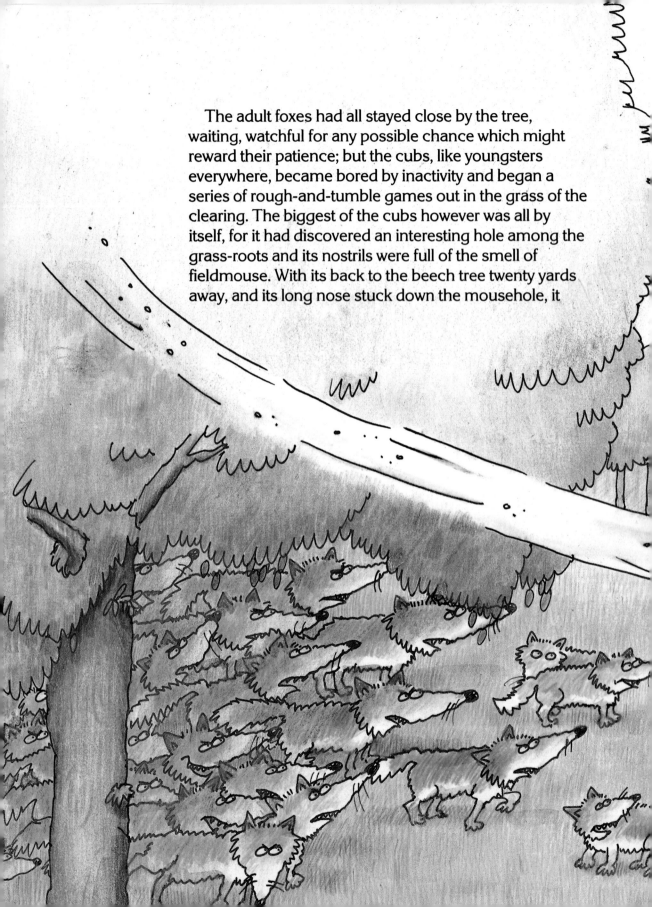

presented to Ransome the perfect target and the perfect final contemptuous gesture towards the foe. She suddenly spread her great wings and flew off her perch like an eagle, diving arrow-straight at the rump of the isolated fox-cub. Such were her powers of acceleration that she was travelling at almost full speed when she hit it, bowling it over and over and leaving it yelping with fright.

She turned and swept once low over the mass of foxes, milling and yapping now in helpless fury, then climbed till the red shapes dwindled, and set course for the farm. The exercise had gone better than she had dared to hope. The fear in her mind had dwindled too.

Written by Dick King-Smith,
illustrated by Frances Cony

JULIUS CAESAR and the ROMAN EMPIRE

Julius Caesar was a Roman general. His army conquered the Gauls in *Gallia* and made *Gallia* part of the Roman Empire.

Countries in the
Roman Empire
55 BC

The people in the empire spoke many different languages in everyday life. But the Romans spoke in **Latin** and wrote their books and laws in Latin. All the names on the map are in Latin.

Ruling the Empire

In Rome, there was a **senate** which was a council of leaders. They decided on the laws and taxes which people in the empire must pay.

The senate sent orders to Roman **governors** who were in charge of the different lands in the empire. Horseriders carried the orders along the stone roads that soldiers had made people build for them.

The Appian Way

You can still see parts of Roman roads today. This one went from Rome to southern Italy.

Roman towns

All over the empire the Romans built towns where soldiers, merchants and governors lived in the same way as people in Rome.

The central forum in Rome

The **forum** in Rome was a place for markets and public meetings. Around the sides were temples, law courts and other public buildings.

An **amphitheatre** was where Romans watched men fighting other men or animals. Today you can see ruins of amphitheatres in many countries.

The Roman amphitheatre in Nimes, France

Julius Caesar knew the Gauls were helped by the people in *Britannia*. The Britons sold them cloth and wheat as well as iron to make swords. So in 55 BC, Julius Caesar brought an army to attack *Britannia*. What kind of people did he find?

The BRITONS

The **Britons** were divided into tribes. Julius Caesar attacked some of the tribes and their kings agreed to live in peace with the Roman Empire. The Romans did not come back to *Britannia* for nearly a hundred years.

Where did the Britons live?

A hill fort

Most Britons lived in family farms and grew corn in tiny square fields. They dried the ears of corn and stored them in holes in the ground. If danger came, they would leave the farm and go to one of their tribe's villages.

Some villages were built in the middle of a lake for safety. Others were on high ground, and we call these **hill forts** because they were protected by a circle of walls and ditches.

Britons at work

Weavers made cloth out of wool coloured with dyes made from soils and plants.

Torcs or neck ornaments made of twisted gold bars

Smiths made goods out of gold, iron or bronze, which is a mixture of copper and tin.

Potters decorated the pots they made from clay.

Druids were the learned men. They advised the kings and gave lessons to the sons of important Britons. They also led worship in sacred places near trees or rivers.

Warrior chiefs wore helmets in battle and painted their faces with a blue dye made from woad plants.

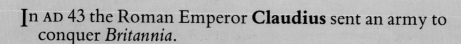

In AD 43 the Roman Emperor **Claudius** sent an army to conquer *Britannia*.

The ROMANS and the BRITONS

Four Roman **legions** came to *Britannia*. The legionaries defeated the tribes in the south of England after four years of fighting.

The Britons defended their forts with **slings**. The Romans used **catapults** to fire iron darts.

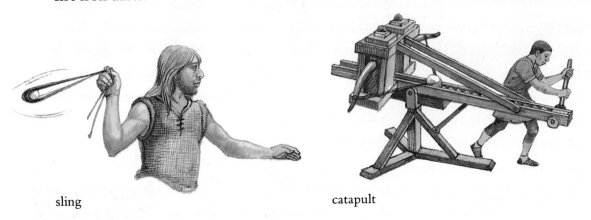

sling   catapult

For a battle, the chiefs of the Britons sent for men and women in farms and villages. They came in carts with their slings and spears. The chiefs rode in chariots. The whole army rushed at the legionaries.

The Roman legionaries made their shields into a wall and waited until the enemy was near. Then they threw their javelins and marched forward to attack with short swords. Then the cavalry charged on horses.

Queen Boudicca

The Romans forced many Britons to work for them to build roads and three big towns. The Romans also collected taxes and corn and cattle to feed their armies. **Boudicca** protested about this. She was queen of the **Iceni** tribe. The Romans flogged her.

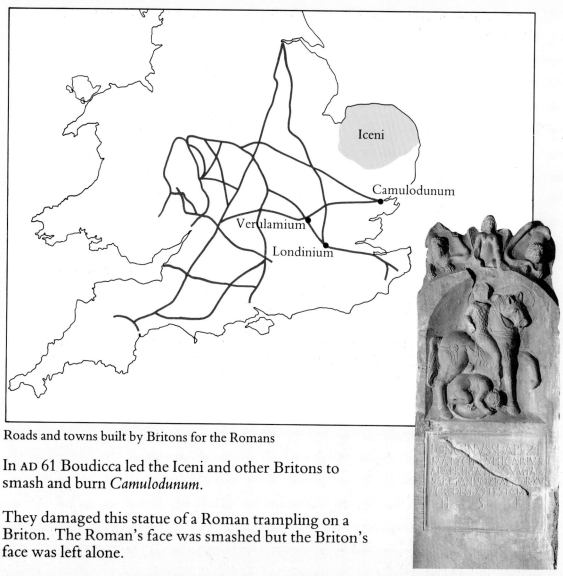

Roads and towns built by Britons for the Romans

In AD 61 Boudicca led the Iceni and other Britons to smash and burn *Camulodunum*.

They damaged this statue of a Roman trampling on a Briton. The Roman's face was smashed but the Briton's face was left alone.

The Roman armies were in Wales. They rushed back after the Iceni had burnt *Camulodunum*, and then *Londinium* and *Verulamium*. Soon afterwards there was a battle. How it ended is told in the story that follows.

Dogs and Wolves and Hares and Foxes

Owain was an orphan, son of a dead noble, and had grown up at the court of Boudicca, the great Warrior Queen. This story tells how he is caught up in the last great struggle of the Ancient Britons against the Roman invaders.

Many weeks after the dreadful day at Queen Boudicca's court, the day he could not bear to remember, Owain found himself in Camulodunum.

He had never seen a town, and his head was dizzy with fever. The streets, the two-storeyed rows of shops, the statues, the hard pavement beneath his feet — all these seemed just another part of the nightmare in which he had been living, and so did not surprise him.

But gradually he became aware that there were people about. Foreign women stood in groups on the pavement, or fingered the glass and pottery on the shelves of the open shops. If they noticed Owain, they wrinkled their noses and drew their skirts aside. Their children stared and pointed. A hard-faced man in a toga shoved past him, and Owain staggered off the pavement almost under the hooves of a Roman farmer's horse. The man swore and raised his whip, and Owain began to run.

He lifted his feet with enormous effort. There was a dark opening in a wall to his left, and a strong fishy smell. He fell towards it, and the world turned upside down.

20

When he opened his eyes he was lying on a gritty floor and someone, a man, was talking in a thick strange accent.

"Dogs and wolves?"

The man bent over Owain. He was fat, with huge red hands, and he had a small sharp iron knife.

"Dogs and wolves?" said the man.

There was another voice, a woman's.

"Let him have a drink."

She held out a clay cup and Owain managed to raise his head to it. It was wine, and it ran warmly down his throat.

"That's better," said the woman. "Now eat."

She brought a bowl of warm barley porridge and fed it to Owain spoonful by spoonful.

"Starving," she said. "Try him now."

"Dogs and wolves?" said the man again. ·

Owain closed his eyes. Nothing made sense, but he didn't care. The woman made an impatient sound.

"Leave him, Julio," she said.

"Throw him out?"

"No," said the woman, after a moment. "Put him in the back. Leave him till Mac comes."

Owain felt himself picked up and carried through a doorway and put down on a heap of fishy-smelling blankets.

"Keep very quiet," said the man. He went out, banging the door, and for the first time since he left Boudicca's land Owain sank fathoms deep into dreamless sleep.

When he woke the fever had gone and his head was clear. It was night. He could see the moon through an opening above his head. He was in a small room with rough plank walls. Barrels and chests were stacked against them, and the floor, when he swung his feet to it, was covered with oyster shells. Through the door he could hear laughter and loud voices, speaking in a language he had heard once before. A sharp pang of fear went through him. He felt weak, and lay back on the rough blankets.

After a long time the voices went away. The door opened and two people came in, one of them carrying a clay lamp. They both bent over Owain, staring intently. The one with the lamp was a boy his own age, with a thin white face and red hair. The other was a girl, obviously his sister. She was wrapped in a plaid cloak and her hair fell in tangles over her face. She had very blue, piercing eyes.

"Dogs and wolves?" It was the boy speaking.

"What?" said Owain.

"He doesn't know the password, Mac," said the girl pleasantly.

"No," agreed Mac. "So we wonder very much who he is and what he's doing here, don't we, Meg."

The girl had a sharp knife, like the one Julio had, and she put it against Owain's wrist.

"Open up, oyster," she said, "Name? Tribe?"

"Owain. Iceni."

"*Iceni*? Your chief is Queen Boudicca? Then why aren't you with her?" The girl seemed excited. "Did you bring a message, did you?"

Owain shook his head. The knife pressed harder and the blue eyes stared into his.

"My father was a Druid," said the girl, "till the Romans killed him. I shall know if you're lying. Whatever you are, spy, traitor, runaway slave — talk."

Against his will, yet in a strange way glad to tell the story, and in any case, unable to help himself while the strange blue eyes held his, Owain began to talk, and time slid backwards.

He was an orphan, son of a dead noble, and he had grown up at Queen Boudicca's court. He had been going to study with the Druids, but there was only one left in the tribe, a very old one, too old to teach. The others had all vanished — gone to the Western Mountains, some said. So Owain stayed at the court, learned to play the harp and memorise poetry, trained his hunting dog Wolf, and sometimes helped with the chariot ponies.

For some time, ever since the old King died, pathetic groups of bewildered peasants — old ones, and women with hungry children — had been coming to Boudicca. They told of bands of fierce foreign soldiers, who had turned them off their farms, stolen the corn, driven away the cattle, and taken the men away in chains, to slavery. Queen Boudicca did her best for them, let them pitch tents nearby, fed them, gave the children milk, let them work in the fields and the woad-gardens if they were able.

Owain watched her as she went among her people. She had aged since her husband's death, and her mass of reddish hair was streaked with grey, her brows drawn together in a permanent heavy frown. But still she was a majestic presence, strong as any warrior. At the councils with her fighting men, which went on far into the night, her voice, raised in anger, could be heard all over the camp.

"What's happening?" Owain said to the blacksmith.

"The Roman invaders," said the blacksmith, spitting. "They're taking over the kingdom."

"But they can't."

"Boy," said the blacksmith. "You live in a world of dreams. The Romans take what they want."

"Can't we fight them?"

"We can," said the blacksmith, "and no doubt we will. But can we win? One tribe, against them all?"

The soldiers came next morning. Owain was watching Elen, the Queen's eldest daughter, combing her yellow hair in the sunshine. Rhian, the youngest girl, held the mirror. Elen was small and gentle, a princess from a bard's song. She wore a green tunic, and her arms when the sleeves fell back were milkwhite.

The soldiers, armed and ferocious, swooped on the camp like a pack of wolves. Great Boudicca herself, striding out to meet them, spear in hand, was seized and flogged, Rhian was clubbed to the ground, and Elen was dragged away, screaming. Now was the time for Owain to hurl himself at her captors and give his life for hers.

But he didn't. He ran away, ran and ran through the forest till he could no longer hear her screams, except in his mind. He had wandered blindly south and at last found that the trees were thinning out, there were roads, then buildings, and he was in Camulodunum.

Mac and Meg listened in silence. Meg took the knife away from Owain's wrist.

"You can't go back," she said. "Because of the shame."

"No," said Owain. "Yes."

"But what if we gave you another chance?" said Mac. "To help your Queen?"

"To help her? But the soldiers —"

"She's not dead. Far from it. Listen."

Mac began to speak urgently, and Owain learned what tremendous things had been happening while he wandered in the forest.

All over south-east England the tribes were gathering. They were going to join together, there was going to be a great rebellion, and Boudicca of the Iceni was the leader.

"The first attack will be on Camulodunum," said Mac. "This town has no defences, no walls or ditches. When the Roman army's out of the way —"

"Out of the way?"

"The Roman governor's taking the legions west, to the mountain country. It's a long, long way. We shall let him get to the mountains, and then we'll rise. By the time he hears of the rebellion, and comes back, it'll be too late."

"And meanwhile," said Meg, "all of us in Camulodunum — all the loyal Britons, I mean, whatever our tribe, have the job of keeping the Roman settlers quiet. Reassuring them. 'Nothing's going to happen. How could the tribes band together and rise against the Romans? We're only savages, but we'd really like to be civilized, like you.' That's what we tell them." She smiled a wolfish smile.

"By day we work for the Romans," said Mac. "Farmworkers, houseboys, nursemaids. And at night we sneak out and meet here, at the back of Julio's Oyster Bar. The settlers come here, you see, to eat and drink and talk, and when they talk, Julio listens. So we know just where the Roman legions are, and when to give the signal to Boudicca. It's important work, Owain. The settlers mustn't know there's trouble coming, or they'll send for help."

Owain nodded.

"So we'll find you a job," Mac went on. "I know a family that needs a houseboy."

Owain nodded again.

"And you'd better know the password," said Meg. "When someone says to you, 'dogs and wolves', you answer 'hares and foxes'. Then you'll know you can trust them. There's plenty of traitors around. 'Dogs and wolves'."

"Hares and foxes," said Owain obediently. "Why?" he added.

"Your Queen spoke those words," said Meg solemnly. "When she spoke to the tribal chiefs at the meeting in the forest, when they planned the rebellion. 'Don't be afraid of the Romans,' she said, 'they're hares and foxes trying to rule dogs and wolves.'"

A strange few weeks followed. Owain didn't forget Elen. But what was done was done, and he could avenge her.

His job with the Roman settlers was unexpectedly easy. True, the farmer was a hard-bitten man who drove the natives with a lash. But Owain worked in the house, and the settler's wife took a fancy to her gentle, sad-eyed servant. He didn't break her precious household goods, he handled the delicate glass and coloured pottery as if he thought they were beautiful. He played with the children, and made them toys, and sang them little crooning songs.

She and her friends met to gossip, and Owain, handing wine and cakes, soon picked up enough Latin to understand what they said. One day he heard his mistress saying, "I don't think there's any danger from the natives. They're just like big children really. All they need is a firm hand. My Owain is so good with the children, and I really think he respects me. He can see what life is like in a civilized house, with baths and drains and proper chairs to sit on. I can't imagine him doing anything to harm us."

Owain smiled to himself. Little did she know. He was acting his part well. And yet — and yet — these were home-sick strangers, like himself; and the children were affectionate and confiding. When Boudicca's army came —

Owain put these thoughts away. The Romans had had no pity for Boudicca or her people. He could not afford pity, either.

He enjoyed the secret meetings after midnight in the dark back room at Julio's. Mac and Meg were his special friends, but he met people from many tribes. Each one of them had a bitter story of stolen land, cruel beatings, arrogant stupid women, harsh masters. These stories united them all, and, because Boudicca's army was growing daily in the forest, their hopes and confidence rose. And the Roman legions were marching across Britain — fifty miles away, a hundred miles away. Soon the hour for rebellion would come.

27

One night a group of the freedom fighters, with Mac and Meg, took Owain round the city. They went to the square where the huge temple of the Emperor Claudius stood, marble pillars gleaming in the moonlight.

"That's where the settlers will go when the fighting starts," said a one-eyed tribesman. "Julio's heard them talking. They'll be safe there. They think."

In front of the temple was a statue of a winged figure, spear in hand, looking out over the roofs of the city.

"What's that?" said Owain.

"They call it the Winged Victory," said Meg. "It's meant to show us excitable savages how ever-victorious the Romans are, or something."

"Let's pull it down," said Owain.

He spoke almost without thinking but the others seized on the idea with glee. Some went off to fetch ropes. Others, led by Meg, took up stations round the temple. Their job was to howl and yell and draw the temple police away.

It worked. The wind had risen and the streets were full of moving shadows. Owain and Mac got the ropes over the wings on the statue, they pulled, it rocked on its plinth, they pulled again, and the Winged Victory fell with a crash to the ground.

The result next day was all they'd hoped for. The settlers were very frightened. Were the gods angry? Did this mean the

gods of victory were withdrawing their protection from Camulodunum?

"It certainly does," said Mac, when he heard this. And then, two nights later, no customers came to the oyster bar. Julio came running into the back room.

"Listen," he said. "It's begun."

Far in the distance, borne on the night wind, came the roar of a mighty army. The British tribes were pouring out of the forest to attack Camulodunum. Yelling, smashing, burning, killing, they swept through the town like a tidal wave.

Owain and Mac and Meg ran and yelled and waved burning torches like the rest. The crowd was surging towards the temple. Mac made for a statue of the Emperor.

"His head, I'll have his head!" he shouted. He hurled himself at the stone plinth, swarmed up it, and wrenched and hacked at the metal head till it came away and he brandished it triumphantly. But this was his undoing. The statue fell, bringing Mac with it. Owain pulled Meg aside, but not quickly enough, and a block of stone fell across her legs. The tribesmen streamed past towards the burning temple, and suddenly Owain and Meg were alone.

He could do nothing for Mac, but he managed to pull the stone off Meg's legs, and drag her to the shelter of a half-burned shop.

When all the settlers had died in the ruins of the temple, and the triumphant rebels had moved on to Verulamium and Londinium, Owain and Meg stayed on in a city of ghosts that stank of blood and death. Very soon, Meg would die too.

Owain bent over her one night and bathed her sweating brow, tried to force wine between her lips. She opened her eyes.

"Mac," she said.

"I'll look after you, Meg."

"No," she said, "I'm dying. But listen, Owain, you'll see your queen again. She passed you while Mac was climbing the statue. You didn't see her. But you will see her again."

Her eyes closed.

"Owain," she said again, "Owain I can see the last battle."

"What can you see Meg? Victory?"

She shuddered. Then she whispered "Victory. The Winged Victory."

She was quiet for a long time, so that Owain thought that she had left him, but she had one more thing to say.

"Owain, after the last battle, go home. Go home to Boudicca's land. You will find her there."

"Who, Meg, who?"

She smiled. "You know."

Then she said, "Dogs and wolves, Owain."

"Hares and foxes, Meg."

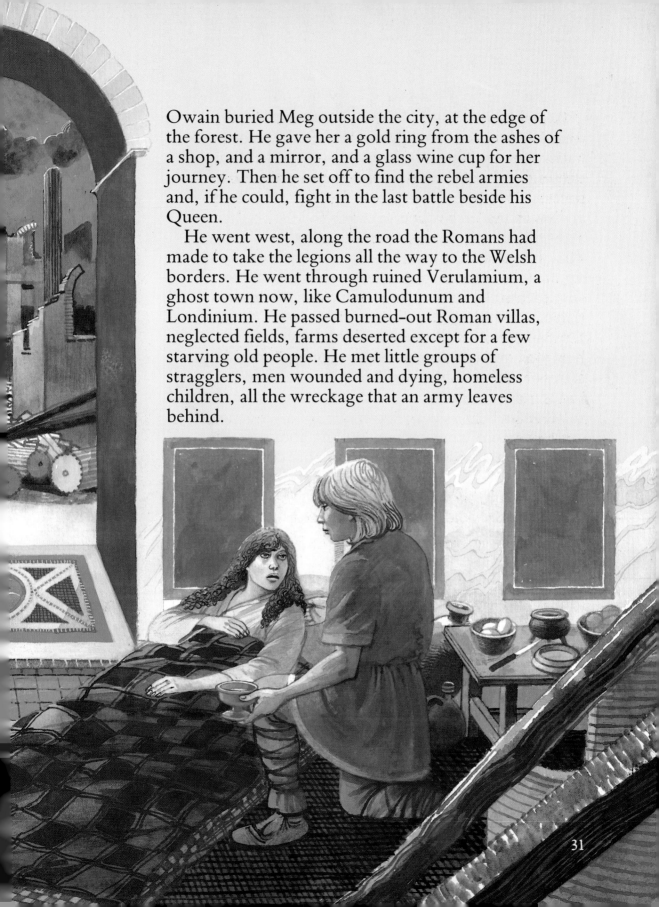

Owain buried Meg outside the city, at the edge of
the forest. He gave her a gold ring from the ashes of
a shop, and a mirror, and a glass wine cup for her
journey. Then he set off to find the rebel armies
and, if he could, fight in the last battle beside his
Queen.

He went west, along the road the Romans had
made to take the legions all the way to the Welsh
borders. He went through ruined Verulamium, a
ghost town now, like Camulodunum and
Londinium. He passed burned-out Roman villas,
neglected fields, farms deserted except for a few
starving old people. He met little groups of
stragglers, men wounded and dying, homeless
children, all the wreckage that an army leaves
behind.

At last Owain found himself climbing through trees to the brow of a hill, and looked down on a narrow valley. There below him — as if, he thought fleetingly, this were a Roman theatre, and he a spectator looking down on a stage — he saw two armies facing each other.

At the narrow western end of the valley, with thick forest at their back, the Romans were drawn up, rank by rank. Legionaries stood shoulder to shoulder in the centre, the cavalry waited on the flanks.

Facing them, at the open end of the valley, but hemmed in by their carts and wagons, was the huge army of the British tribesmen. There seemed thousands and thousands of them, many more than the Romans.

The Britons were yelling, milling about, waving their spears, shouting insults and defiance. But the Romans stood like a wall, grimly silent, waiting.

Owain knew, with a cold certainty, that this would indeed be the last battle. He didn't have to fight. He could go back now, by the forest paths, to Iceni land, to Boudicca's kingdom.

But if he found Elen again, and she said, "Tell me how you fought for your Queen," and he had to say, "I wasn't there, I didn't fight"?

No. Better death and the happy land. Owain had no weapon but he picked up a piece of wood for a club and ran down the hill through the trees, to his tribesmen. And then he saw Boudicca.

She stood in her chariot in front of her army and her cloak flew out in the wind, like wings. "The Winged Victory," thought Owain. He pushed through the mob and stood at her chariot wheel. She looked down and saw him, and smiled. Then she shouted,

"Oh British dogs and wolves, we are thousands, they are hundreds. Remember what you're fighting for. Make them run. One last battle and our country will be free for ever! Now! Charge!"

The chariot-driver lashed the horses and wheeled sideways as the tribesmen started forward, so that the Queen could see what was happening and direct the attack. The Roman army waited till the Britons were within arm's length; then they hurled their javelins, and then they were fighting hand to hand, and Owain with them, and as the Roman bugles rang out, and the cavalry began to press from the side, step by desperate step, the vast British army was driven back by the irresistible force of the Roman legionaries, until, entangled in its own carts and wagons, it was cut to pieces.

Many weeks later Owain limped up the overgrown path to the Queen's dwelling-hall, catching his feet in the brambles, grasping painfully at thorny branches which tore at his ragged cloak.

He picked his way past a rusted plough, a heap of broken pots, a twisted chariot wheel, to the great door that swung creaking on sagging hinges. He pushed it open.

Nettles were growing through the floor and spiders had spun diamond webs from corner to corner of the rafters. In the central hearth the ashes were cold. A harp with broken strings lay in the dust. Owain trembled with cold and pain. The gash in his leg was bleeding again. Slowly and painfully he went outside and gathered dry leaves and twigs. He fumbled in the pouch at his belt and struck flint against ironstone till the tinder caught. Presently flames leaped from the ashes and thin smoke began to spiral through the roof-hole.

Owain sat down by the fire and waited. A whimper roused him, and a cold muzzle pressed into his hand.

"Wolf," he said. The hunting dog whined and pressed closer and he stroked it. "Wolf, where is she?"

Wolf pricked his ears and turned his head to the door. Owain heard it creak open, then dragging footsteps came slowly across the floor.

He looked up, and there she was. Ragged and thin, infinitely worn, golden hair dulled and green tunic torn and stained, white hands rough and red.

"Elen," he said.

"The soldiers took me away," she said, almost pleadingly. "I escaped. I lived in the woods."

"Come and get warm," said Owain, But she stood and looked at him.

"My mother? She's dead, isn't she."

"Yes," said Owain. "After the last battle, when the Romans beat us, she went away and poisoned herself."

"So it's all over."

"Yes," said Owain. "It's over."

"But you won't go away?"

He looked at her, and beyond her, through the open door to the empty courtyard, the fields of rotting corn, the weeds growing in the woad-gardens.

"No," he said. "I won't run away. We'll survive, Elen. We'll survive."

Written by Margery Morris, illustrated by Clyde Pearson

Saturday was warm and bright, the first pretty Saturday they had had since Christmas. Mouse, lying on his bed in the hall, could tell it was sunny just from the brightness of the normally dark hall.

"Mom!" he called, not knowing what time it was and whether she had gone out to deliver cosmetics yet. "Mom!" There was no answer. There used to be a boy who lived in the apartment next door when Mouse was little, and every time Mouse would call, "Mommie!" the boy would answer, "Whatie?" in a high false voice.

Mouse got out of bed slowly, in stages. He sat on the edge of the bed, leaned forward, looked at his feet, straightened, and then continued to stand by the bed for a moment. Then abruptly he dressed, went into the kitchen and looked at the boxes of cereal on the shelf. He tore open a box of Sugar Pops. He waited, looking at the cereal, and then refolded the box and put it back. He went into the living-room, and out of habit he switched on the television. Superman was on the screen, flying over the city in his suit and cape. Mouse watched for a moment and then turned off the television. Superman might be faster than a speeding bullet and able to leap tall buildings with a single bound, Mouse thought, but even Superman couldn't keep himself from being turned down to a small white dot.

Mouse got his jacket from the chair by the door. Even though he knew it was going to be warm outside, he put on his jacket and zipped it up. Then he left the apartment.

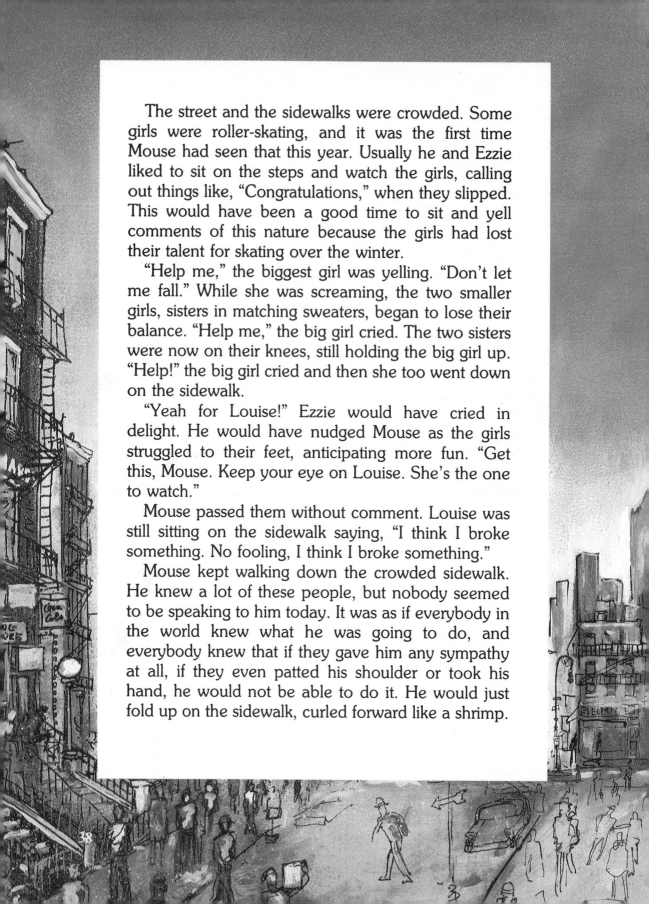

The street and the sidewalks were crowded. Some girls were roller-skating, and it was the first time Mouse had seen that this year. Usually he and Ezzie liked to sit on the steps and watch the girls, calling out things like, "Congratulations," when they slipped. This would have been a good time to sit and yell comments of this nature because the girls had lost their talent for skating over the winter.

"Help me," the biggest girl was yelling. "Don't let me fall." While she was screaming, the two smaller girls, sisters in matching sweaters, began to lose their balance. "Help me," the big girl cried. The two sisters were now on their knees, still holding the big girl up. "Help!" the big girl cried and then she too went down on the sidewalk.

"Yeah for Louise!" Ezzie would have cried in delight. He would have nudged Mouse as the girls struggled to their feet, anticipating more fun. "Get this, Mouse. Keep your eye on Louise. She's the one to watch."

Mouse passed them without comment. Louise was still sitting on the sidewalk saying, "I think I broke something. No fooling, I think I broke something."

Mouse kept walking down the crowded sidewalk. He knew a lot of these people, but nobody seemed to be speaking to him today. It was as if everybody in the world knew what he was going to do, and everybody knew that if they gave him any sympathy at all, if they even patted his shoulder or took his hand, he would not be able to do it. He would just fold up on the sidewalk, curled forward like a shrimp.

He crossed the street, touching both feet on the old trolley tracks because this was supposed to bring luck, and he stepped up on the sidewalk in front of the laundry. He thought that he could walk down this street blindfold and know right where he was. The odours that came out of the different doors told him what to expect, what cracks there were in the sidewalk, who would be standing in the doorways. He turned the corner, passed the old movie theatre, the Rialto. He smelled the old musty smell. Then he stopped thinking of anything except the fact that he was now on Marv Hammerman's street.

A bus passed him, stopped to pick up an old woman with a folded shopping bag under her arm and then moved on. Mouse had started to sweat. It wasn't that warm a day, not even with his jacket zipped up, but sweat was running down his sides beneath his shirt in a way it had never done before. At the same time his throat had gone completely dry, and the two conditions seemed somehow connected.

He saw a boy who had been in his school last year and he asked, "Have you seen Marv Hammerman?" His voice had the crackling dry sound of old leaves. He turned his head away and coughed.

"Not this morning."

"Doesn't he live around here?"

"He lives right over there," the boy said. "Lots of times he's down at Stumpy's."

"Oh."

"If I see him I'll tell him you're looking for him."

"I'm Mouse Fawley," he said, looking at the boy, and the boy said, "I know."

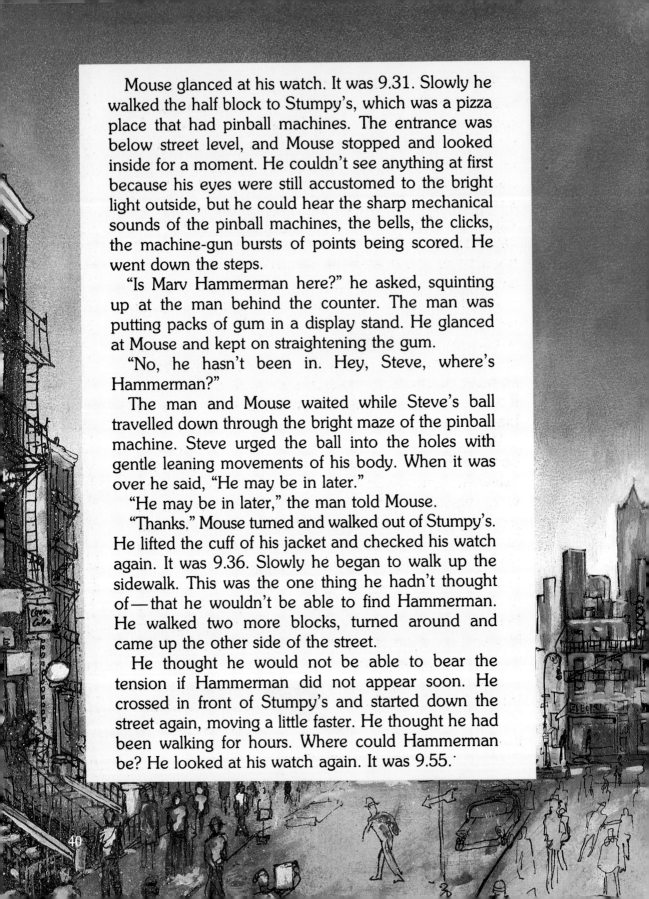

Mouse glanced at his watch. It was 9.31. Slowly he walked the half block to Stumpy's, which was a pizza place that had pinball machines. The entrance was below street level, and Mouse stopped and looked inside for a moment. He couldn't see anything at first because his eyes were still accustomed to the bright light outside, but he could hear the sharp mechanical sounds of the pinball machines, the bells, the clicks, the machine-gun bursts of points being scored. He went down the steps.

"Is Marv Hammerman here?" he asked, squinting up at the man behind the counter. The man was putting packs of gum in a display stand. He glanced at Mouse and kept on straightening the gum.

"No, he hasn't been in. Hey, Steve, where's Hammerman?"

The man and Mouse waited while Steve's ball travelled down through the bright maze of the pinball machine. Steve urged the ball into the holes with gentle leaning movements of his body. When it was over he said, "He may be in later."

"He may be in later," the man told Mouse.

"Thanks." Mouse turned and walked out of Stumpy's. He lifted the cuff of his jacket and checked his watch again. It was 9.36. Slowly he began to walk up the sidewalk. This was the one thing he hadn't thought of — that he wouldn't be able to find Hammerman. He walked two more blocks, turned around and came up the other side of the street.

He thought he would not be able to bear the tension if Hammerman did not appear soon. He crossed in front of Stumpy's and started down the street again, moving a little faster. He thought he had been walking for hours. Where could Hammerman be? He looked at his watch again. It was 9.55.

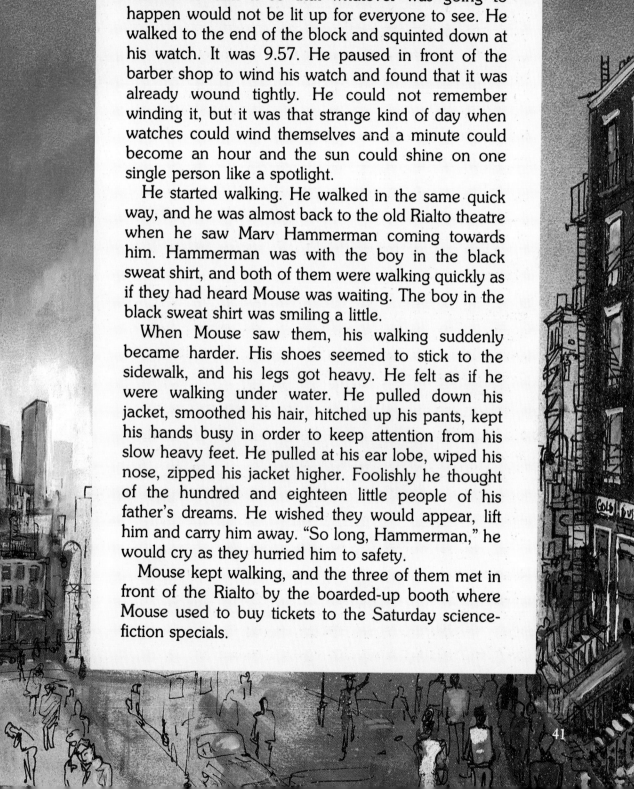

The sunlight seemed blinding now, and Mouse wanted to dim it so that whatever was going to happen would not be lit up for everyone to see. He walked to the end of the block and squinted down at his watch. It was 9.57. He paused in front of the barber shop to wind his watch and found that it was already wound tightly. He could not remember winding it, but it was that strange kind of day when watches could wind themselves and a minute could become an hour and the sun could shine on one single person like a spotlight.

He started walking. He walked in the same quick way, and he was almost back to the old Rialto theatre when he saw Marv Hammerman coming towards him. Hammerman was with the boy in the black sweat shirt, and both of them were walking quickly as if they had heard Mouse was waiting. The boy in the black sweat shirt was smiling a little.

When Mouse saw them, his walking suddenly became harder. His shoes seemed to stick to the sidewalk, and his legs got heavy. He felt as if he were walking under water. He pulled down his jacket, smoothed his hair, hitched up his pants, kept his hands busy in order to keep attention from his slow heavy feet. He pulled at his ear lobe, wiped his nose, zipped his jacket higher. Foolishly he thought of the hundred and eighteen little people of his father's dreams. He wished they would appear, lift him and carry him away. "So long, Hammerman," he would cry as they hurried him to safety.

Mouse kept walking, and the three of them met in front of the Rialto by the boarded-up booth where Mouse used to buy tickets to the Saturday science-fiction specials.

Mouse finished working the zipper on his jacket and pulled his cuffs down. He said to Hammerman, "I was sick yesterday and I had to go home, but I'm here now."

It came out in a rush. Mouse hoped that he hadn't said it so quickly that Hammerman didn't hear it. It was important that this one thing be said while he was still able to talk.

"He still looks a little sick to me, don't he to you?" the boy in the black sweat shirt said, smiling. "Course he looks better than he's *gonna* look."

Mouse didn't say anything. He was trying to steel himself for the battle. The only thing he knew about fighting, he realized now, was that if you put your thumbs inside your fists and hit somebody hard with your hand like that, you could break your thumb. He rearranged his hands which he had instinctively folded with the thumbs inside.

He cleared his throat, wondering if he was supposed to say something else. He had had so little experience in fighting that he did not know how a fight of this kind, an arranged fight, would actually start. He remembered seeing a fist fight in an old silent movie on television one time, and the opponents had lifted their fists at the same moment, in the same position, and had circled each other in a set pattern. Still he couldn't imagine this fight starting, not in that way or any other. He could only imagine the ending.

The boy in the black sweat shirt jerked his head at Hammerman. He said to Mouse, "He don't like anybody writing things about him."

Mouse was so nervous he thought perhaps the boy

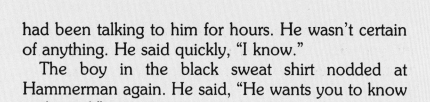

had been talking to him for hours. He wasn't certain of anything. He said quickly, "I know."

The boy in the black sweat shirt nodded at Hammerman again. He said, "He wants you to know real good."

The sun went behind a cloud, and it was suddenly dim beneath the marquee. Mouse couldn't see for a minute. He had been looking at the boy in the sweat shirt while he was talking, and now the boy was silent. All Mouse could see was the whiteness of his smile.

Mouse looked back at Hammerman. For a moment he couldn't see him clearly either. Hammerman's face was a pale circle in the darkness, like the children's faces in the hospital ward, lit up by the light from Mouse's flashlight. Then, abruptly, everything snapped into focus. Hammerman's face was so clear there seemed to be nothing between Mouse and Hammerman, not even air. They could have been up in that high altitude area where the air thins and even distant points come into focus.

Hammerman hadn't made a move that Mouse could see. He was still standing with his hands at his sides, his feet apart. But his body had lost its relaxed look and was ready in a way that Mouse's body would never be.

Mouse raised his fists. His thumbs were carefully outside, pointing upward so that he appeared to be handling invisible controls of some sort. Then he saw Hammerman's fist coming towards him, the knuckles like pale pecans, and at the same time Mouse saw Hammerman's eyes, pale also but very bright. Then Hammerman's fist slammed into his stomach.

Mouse doubled over and staggered backwards a few steps. He thought for a moment that he was going to fall to the ground, just sit down like a baby who has lost his balance. He didn't, and after a second he straightened and came towards Hammerman. He threw out his right hand.

He didn't see Hammerman's fist this time, just felt it in the stomach again. It was so hard that Mouse made a strangled noise. If he had eaten breakfast, there would have been Sugar Pops all over the sidewalk from that blow.

Choking, coughing, he staggered all the way back and hit against the side of the theatre where pictures of man-made monsters used to be posted. He stayed there a minute, bent over his stomach, waiting for his strength to return. He could almost feel the old favourites — Gorgo, Mothra, Godzilla. He felt for a minute that he had become glued to the theatre, plastered there like the pictured monsters. Then he came free and took three heavy steps forward to where Hammerman was waiting. Gorgo had walked like this. Mouse thought of how Gorgo's feet had crushed whole buildings with these same heavy steps. His own feet could barely lift the weight of a pair of tennis shoes.

Mouse's hands were up. He threw the invisible controls forward and hit nothing. Then he felt a sharp stinging blow on his breastbone. He hadn't seen that one coming either. He put out his fists to ward off blows again rather than to land them, and then Hammerman's fist was in his face. It landed somehow on his nose and mouth at the same time. Then there was another blow directly on his nose.

Mouse's nose began to gush blood. The blood seemed to be coming from everywhere, not just the nose, and Mouse wiped his face with one hand. Quickly, anxiously he got his hands back in position. He threw the right control forward.

Suddenly he couldn't see. He wiped his hand over his eyes, then wiped his nose and got set. He was leaning forward now, pressing his knees together to steady them. The blood from his nose was splattering on the sidewalk.

He waited, wondering how long he could continue to hold this position. Then he heard Hammerman say, "You had enough?"

"No, he hasn't had enough," the boy in the black sweat shirt said. "He's still standing."

Hammerman said again. "You had enough?"

Hammerman's voice seemed to be coming from somewhere far away, but the voice wasn't asking the right question, Mouse thought. It seemed simple suddenly. He saw it now as an old-fashioned matter of honour. He, Mouse, had dishonoured Marv Hammerman; and now Hammerman had to be the one to say when his honour was restored. It was one of those things that doesn't become absolutely clear until the last minute and then becomes so clear it dazzles the mind.

Mouse could hear Dick Fellini's voice explaining honour and knighthood to the English class. He could hear Ezzie saying, "Ask me anything you want to about honour, Mr Stein, and I'll tell you." It was an odd thing but he, Mouse, who had felt honour, who had been run through with it like a sword, couldn't say a word about it.

He looked at Hammerman, squinting at him, and said, "If you have."

"If *he* has!" the boy in the black sweat shirt cried. "Man, he can keep going like this all morning."

There was a long pause, and Mouse suddenly feared he was going to start crying. He couldn't understand why he should want to cry now when it was almost over. The worst thing that could happen now was the big final blow, the knock-out punch that would leave him unconscious in the shadow of the Rialto. He could even take that if only he did not start crying.

Hammerman lifted one hand and opened it a little as if he were releasing something. It was a strange gesture, and it seemed to Mouse the kind of gesture a dancer might try to make, or a painter might try to put in a picture. He imagined a small statue, bronze, on a round pedestal, of Marv Hammerman with his partially raised open hand.

Hammerman said, "Go on."

"What?"

"Go on."

Mouse wiped his nose with the back of his hand and said, "Thank you."

The boy in the black sweat shirt leaned back and hollered, "Whoooo-eeee! You welcome."

Mouse passed them, holding his hand over his nose. The boy in the sweat shirt laughed again. It was a loud explosive laugh, and the boy spun around to watch Mouse walk away.

"Whooo-eeee!" he said. "You are most certainly welcome. Come around anytime."

Mouse turned the corner and kept walking. Tears were in his eyes now, and he could not see where he was going. It was, he thought, the gesture that had weakened him. The careless ease of that opened hand — Mouse couldn't seem to get that out of his mind.

He made his way down the sidewalk with his eyes closed. He thought suddenly that if he could see where he was going it would probably not be down Fourth Street at all. He was probably walking across some dusty foreign field. If he could look up, he would not see the tops of buildings, the flat blue sky with a jet trail drawn across it. He would see gold and scarlet tournament flags snapping in the wind. There would be plumes and trumpets and horses in bright trappings. Honour would be a simple thing again and so vital that people would talk of it wherever they went.

He felt as if a vanished age had risen up like a huge wave and washed over him. Then he smelled a dry starchy smell and knew he was passing the laundry. He stopped and wiped his hand across his eyes to clear them. He stepped against the wall and then opened the door into an apartment building where he didn't know anybody. He sank down on the steps against the wall.

With a sigh he hung his head and pinched his nose shut. His nose was still bleeding. He saw that now. He noticed the other damage. His upper lip was bleeding and starting to swell. His stomach hurt so bad it might be weeks before it would accept food again. He couldn't bend over any further without feeling the pain in his breastbone. He looked at his watch. It was 10.13.

Well, he thought wryly, at least I didn't break my thumbs.

Written by Betsy Byars,
illustrated by Chris Price

BETSY BYARS

Betsy Byars was born on 7th August 1928, in Charlotte, North Carolina, in the United States of America. She now lives in Morgantown, West Virginia.

San Francisco

Los Angeles

Morgantown

New Y

West Virginia

Virginia

North Carolina Charlotte

Betsy Byars started writing books for children as her own family grew up and started to enjoy reading stories for themselves.

When she talks about writing her many popular children's stories, Betsy Byars explains that her books usually begin with something that has really happened like a newspaper story, or an event from her own children's lives.

It takes Betsy Byars about a year to write a book, but after that she spends another full year thinking about it further and polishing it.

Living with her own teenage children and listening to them taught Betsy that she must not write down to her readers. She says:

> "Boys and girls are very sharp today, and when I visit classrooms to talk with students, I am impressed to find that many of them are writing stories, and how knowledgeable they are about writing."

Here are some of Betsy Byars' most famous books

Betsy Byars has written a lot more books that you will probably enjoy reading when you are older.

51

HOW FAR TO China?

A true story of long ago written by **Pat Edwards** and illustrated by **Peter Foster**.

Botany Bay 1791

I BELIEVE YOU KNOW SOMETHING ABOUT FISHING, WILLIAM BRYANT!

AYE, SIR. MORE THAN THE OFFICERS DO. WE'LL ALL STARVE IF WE HAVE TO RELY ON WHAT THEY CATCH.

Botany Bay: a place in Australia where convicts were kept.

William went back to work, his mind full of plans.

William's plan grew day by day.

William did get caught, and he was flogged. But that didn't stop him.

William told seven other convicts of his plan to steal away in the Governor's boat.

55

The long trip began...

EVERYONE RECKONED IT'S NOT THAT FAR TO CHINA, JOHN.

AH, SAMUEL, ANYWHERE THAT'S NOT THIS ROTTEN COUNTRY WILL DO ME.

... but so did the nightmare. They soon used up their supplies.

BUT WILLIAM, IT'S EMMANUEL'S FIRST BIRTHDAY. CAN'T I GIVE HIM JUST A LITTLE WATER?

And the Australian coast seemed to go on forever.

DADDY, HOW FAR TO CHINA?

STOP PESTERING, CHARLOTTE!

HUSH, WILLIAM. SHE'S ONLY THREE.

They were forced to go ashore to hunt for food and water.

JAMES AND SAMUEL, YOU LOOK FOR WATER. NATHANIEL AND JOHN, YOU COME HUNTING WITH ME.

WATCH OUT FOR NATIVES, WILLIAM.

WE'LL CHECK THE SHIP, WILLIAM.

There were fierce storms...

KEEP BAILING OR WE'LL SINK!

DADDY, HOW FAR IS IT TO CHINA?

HUSH, CHARLOTTE!

and always the fear of capture.

WE DAREN'T LAND HERE. THOSE ABORIGINES LOOK ANGRY.

BUT WE'RE DESPERATELY SHORT OF WATER!

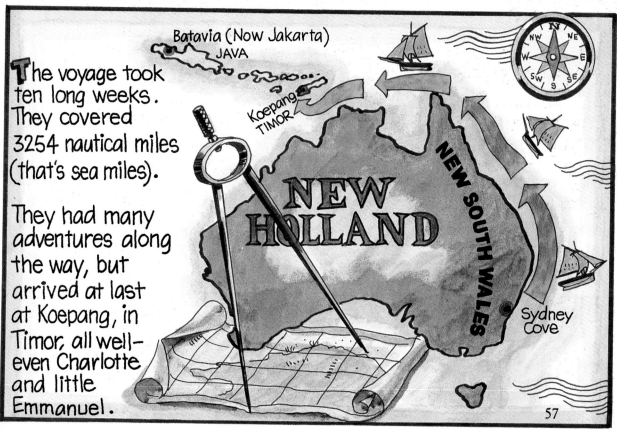

The voyage took ten long weeks. They covered 3254 nautical miles (that's sea miles).

They had many adventures along the way, but arrived at last at Koepang, in Timor, all well— even Charlotte and little Emmanuel.

Batavia (Now Jakarta)
JAVA
Koepang
TIMOR
NEW HOLLAND
NEW SOUTH WALES
Sydney Cove

June 5, 1791

WE HAVE TO THINK OF A STORY! THEY MUST NEVER KNOW WE'RE ESCAPED CONVICTS.

William had already thought of one.

WE'LL TELL THEM THAT WE WERE SHIP-WRECKED AND THAT EVERYONE ELSE WAS DROWNED.

REMEMBER— WE'VE NEVER BEEN ANYWHERE NEAR AUSTRALIA. WE CAME STRAIGHT FROM ENGLAND!

WELL, MARY, IT SEEMS WE'RE IN A PLACE CALLED KOEPANG. THEY SAY WE CAN STAY FOR A TIME.

MAYBE WE'LL EVEN GET TO ENGLAND ONE DAY!

IT SEEMS TOO GOOD TO BE TRUE, WILL.

58

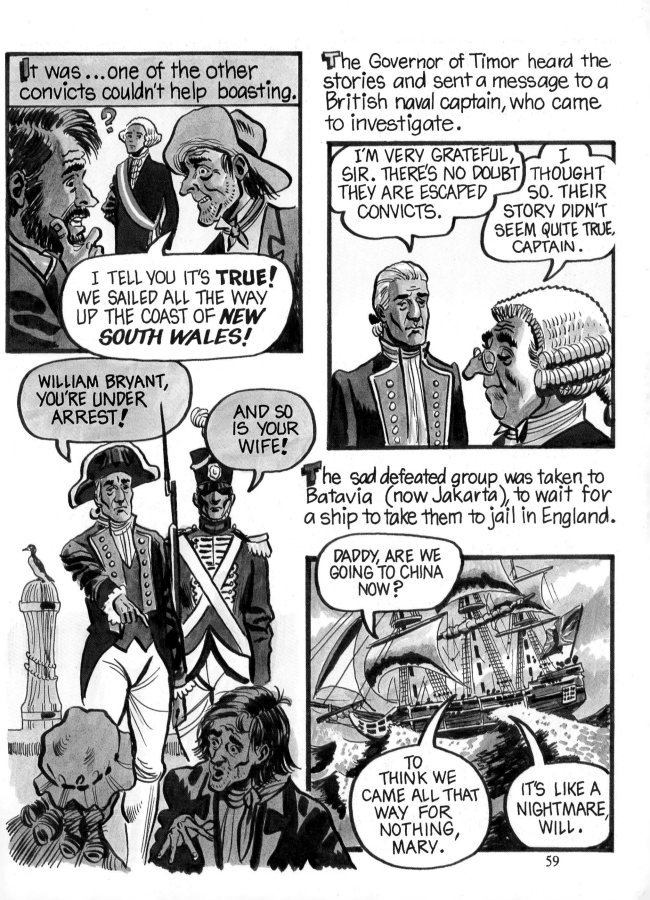

And at Batavia, the nightmare got worse.

I FEEL REALLY ILL, MARY.

EMMANUEL IS VERY SICK, TOO. THEY SAY THE FEVER IS BAD IN THE PORT.

William and Emmanuel both died.

THE CAPTAIN LET US COME TO SAY HOW SORRY WE ARE, MARY.

OH, SAMUEL! WHAT IS TO BECOME OF US?

MUM, I FEEL SICK.

At last the ship for England was ready to sail.

HURRY UP, YOU CONVICTS. WE SAIL WITH THE TIDE.

LET ME CARRY CHARLOTTE, MARY.

PERHAPS THE SEA AIR WILL MAKE HER BETTER.

But Charlotte didn't get better.

SHE'S **DEAD**— MY LITTLE GIRL IS DEAD! OH, WHEN WILL THE NIGHTMARE END?

SAMUEL AND JOHN ARE BOTH DEAD, TOO!

On went the ship to England with more tragedy to come.

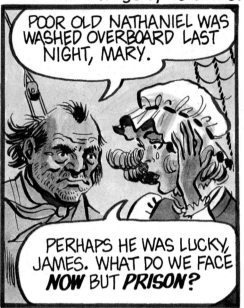

POOR OLD NATHANIEL WAS WASHED OVERBOARD LAST NIGHT, MARY.

PERHAPS HE WAS LUCKY, JAMES. WHAT DO WE FACE **NOW** BUT **PRISON?**

They arrived back in London. It was 1792 and the four survivors were tried again.

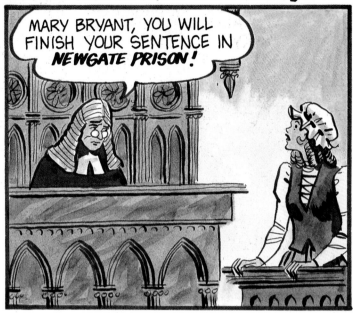

MARY BRYANT, YOU WILL FINISH YOUR SENTENCE IN *NEWGATE PRISON!*

But at last Mary's luck turned. A man named James Boswell heard of the escape and decided to help Mary and the others.

Thanks to him, they were all allowed to go free the next year.

James Boswell paid Mary ten pounds a year for the rest of her life.

It was enough to live on in those days.

Mary was only 28 years old when she came out of prison. No one knows the end of her story.

OH, WILLIAM, CHARLOTTE, EMMANUEL ...IF ONLY YOU COULD BE WITH ME NOW!

Talking of nightmares, it isn't only human
children who have them, it seems ...

I don't believe in Human-Tales

I don't believe there's such a thing
As nasty little boys.
I think someone dreams them up;
It's one of the gnome-up's ploys.

I don't believe in super-stores
Where bits of wings and legs
Of harmless little chickens
Are sold in plastic bags.

I'm sure it is just rubbish
That we get turned to stone
If we go near garden ponds
When we're playing out alone.

I'm sure gnome-ups invent these things
To scare us little gnomes
So we'll never leave the forests
Under which we have our homes.

Brian Patten

some  words

Glossary

abruptly (*p. 36*)
all of a sudden

anticipating (*p. 38*)
looking forward to

bard (*p. 24*)
a poet-singer, who
sang about heroes

bewildered (*p. 23*)
confused

brandished (*p. 29*)
waved about

bugles (*p. 33*)
small instruments
like horns, used
in armies, to
call soldiers

catapults (*p. 18*)
machines for
hurling rocks

conceited (*p. 6*)
having a very
high opinion of
yourself

contempt (*p. 10*)
scorn

dwindled (*p. 13*)
became smaller

earth (*p. 10*)
the tunnels that
a fox lives in

fathom (*p. 21*)
a unit of length
equal to 6ft
(1.83 metres) used
for measuring the
depth of water

flanks (*p. 32*)
sides

flogged (*p. 19*)
beat with a
stick or whip

foe (*p. 13*)
enemy

Hennish (*p. 10*)
the language
spoken by
hens

63

Glossary continues on page 64

some more

NIGHTMARISH
words

impudence (*p. 11*)
boldness

lashed (*p. 33*)
hit with a whip

legend (*p. 6*)
a story about the
things done by great
people in the past

manoeuvrability (*p. 7*)
ability to move
quickly in any
direction

marquee (*p. 43*)
large tent or
shelter

mesmerised (*p. 9*)
fixed as if
hypnotised, unable
to move

musty (*p. 39*)
smelling of damp
and mould

nautical miles (*p. 57*)
miles at sea – a
mile on land is a
little longer than
1½ kilometres;
a nautical mile is
about 200 metres
longer than a
land mile

pecans (*p. 43*)
smooth oblong
thin-shelled nuts

plaid (*p. 22*)
material with a
tartan pattern

plinth (*p. 28*)
base of the statue

pullet (*p. 9*)
a young hen

roost-time (*p. 7*)
time when birds come
together ready to
go to sleep

shrewdness (*p. 6*)
cleverness

slings (*p. 18*)
short straps used
for throwing stones

toga (*p. 20*)
a long loose piece
of clothing worn
by the Romans

vixen (*p. 6*)
female fox

Vulpine (*p. 10*)
the language spoken
by foxes

woad (*p. 17*)
a plant which gives
blue dye

wryly (*p. 48*)
in a grim but
humorous
way